Department of H

CHILLED AND FROZEN

Guidelines on Cook-Chill and Cook-Freeze Catering Systems

London: Her Majesty's Stationery Office

© Crown copyright 1989
First published 1989

ISBN 0 11 321161 9

CONTENTS

Chapter	Title	Page
1	INTRODUCTION	1
2	BASIC PRINCIPLES OF THE SYSTEM	3
3	DESCRIPTION OF THE SYSTEM	4
4	NUTRITION AND FLAVOUR EFFECTS	6
5	RAW MATERIALS	8
6	PREPARATION AND STORAGE BEFORE COOKING	9
7	THE COOKING PROCESS	11
8	PREPARATION OF COOKED FOOD FOR CHILLING OR FREEZING	12
9	COOK-CHILL: THE CHILLING PROCESS	14
10	STORAGE OF CHILLED FOOD	17
11	TIME AND TEMPERATURE LIMITATIONS IN STORAGE AND DISTRIBUTION OF CHILLED FOODS	19
12	COOK-FREEZE: THE FREEZING PROCESS	20
13	STORAGE OF PRE-COOKED FROZEN FOODS	21
14	DISTRIBUTION OF PRE-COOKED CHILLED AND PRE-COOKED FROZEN FOOD	22
15	REHEATING AND SERVICE	24
16	MANAGEMENT OF QUALITY ASSURANCE	26
17	MAINTENANCE	30
	BIBLIOGRAPHY	31

FOREWORD

In 1970, the Department produced Guidelines on Pre-Cooked Frozen Foods. Following technological advances, guidelines on Pre-Cooked Chilled Foods were produced in 1980. In the light of developments since publication of these two Guidelines and the growing interest in the Cook-chill system of catering, the Department set up a Working Group to review these two publications.

The Working Group reviewed the detailed operational procedures set out in the Guidelines and took account of users' experience of the systems. It concluded that no changes were necessary in the temperatures recommended for each stage of the systems. However, it was agreed that certain aspects needed clarification and emphasis such as pre-planning, management, distribution and serving. In addition, the two sets of Guidelines have been combined and updated where necessary.

The review included consideration of scientific data from both long established and more recently established Cook-chill catering units and took account of relevant published scientific papers.

Decisions to introduce Cook-chill catering systems are taken by commercial or institutional managers in the light of local catering needs. The design of each system including its cost effectiveness, must relate to those needs.

I should like to thank all of those who have assisted in the preparation of the Guidelines including the members of the Working Group from outside the Department.

The Guidelines will be kept under review.

DONALD ACHESON
CHIEF MEDICAL OFFICER

ACKNOWLEDGEMENTS

WORKING GROUP

Dr R Gilbert	Public Health Laboratory Service
Professor G Glew	Huddersfield Polytechnic
Dr N Light	Dorset Institute of Higher Education
Dr D Smith	Formerly of Dorset Institute of Higher Education
Dr M Stringer	Campden Food and Drink Research Association
Dr P Wilkinson	Public Health Laboratory Service, Plymouth
Mr I Adams	Ministry of Agriculture, Fisheries and Food
Mr R Brown	Department of Health
Mr E Kingcott	Department of Health
Dr H Murrell	Department of Health
Mr R Wenlock	Department of Health
Dr M Wiseman	Department of Health
Miss E Young	Formerly of Department of Health
Mr J Glover	Secretariat — Department of Health

1 INTRODUCTION

1.1 These Guidelines combine and update the Department's existing guidance on pre-cooked chilled foods and pre-cooked frozen foods. They apply only to catering operations; ie. to activities involving the production and service of meals using either of the systems whether or not the meals are consumed at the place of production. They do not give guidance on chilled foods produced under special conditions using processes and packaging designed to provide an expected shelf-life of more than five days.

1.2 Both the cook-chill and cook-freeze systems can give increased flexibility in the preparation and service of meals. They are regarded as satisfactory for use in hospitals, other forms of institutional catering, including meals on wheels and "special function" catering, and in commercial catering provided that the basic principles in this document and other good catering practices are carefully followed at all times. Catering installations are likely to use these systems for part of their total output of meals.

1.3 The Guidelines do not deal in detail with general or personal aspects of food hygiene. However, it is essential that the highest standards of hygiene are maintained at every stage of the operation. The systems must comply with the requirements of the food hygiene regulations*. Before any staff are deployed on these systems they must be given specific training on all food hygiene aspects of the operation. This training should be repeated and updated at appropriate intervals and its effectiveness monitored. The local environmental health department and other competent bodies should be able to advise on suitable training.

*See Bibliography

1.4 If it is decided to use one or both of these systems then the local environmental health department should be involved at the planning stage. Also it is essential that suitable scientific and technical expertise is available either from within the organisation operating the system or, if this is not available, from suitably qualified consultants. In the case of hospitals the control of infection officer and/or microbiologist should be consulted.

1.5 Pre-planning is an essential factor in achieving successful cook-chill and cook-freeze operations. It is strongly recommended that the following in particular should be considered in detail when planning a system:— suitability of existing buildings for conversion; food to be produced; special equipment required including bulk cooking, refrigeration and reheating equipment; design of central production unit and satellite unit; food distribution; hazard analysis; quality assurance and staff training.

2 BASIC PRINCIPLES OF THE SYSTEMS

2.1 The basic principles of the cook-chill and cook-freeze systems are:

- all raw materials should be of good microbiological quality;

- cooking should ensure the destruction of the vegetative stages of any pathogenic micro-organisms present;

- post-cooking rapid chilling or freezing should control growth of micro-organisms;

- cross contamination should be avoided at all stages particularly between raw and cooked food;

- storage and distribution conditions for cooked food should ensure its quality and safety;

- reheating and service procedures should ensure the food's safety and are crucial to its palatability; they should be very carefully monitored.

2.2 This document gives detailed recommendations, in terms of times, temperatures and other operating requirements, to give effect to these basic principles. Any proposal(s) to adopt alternative procedures (eg because of the use of new technology) should be discussed and agreed with the appropriate experts referred to at 1.4 above.

3 DESCRIPTION OF THE SYSTEMS

3.1   The differences between cook-chill and cook-freeze must be clearly understood, particularly in operations where a mixture of cook-chill and cook-freeze product is produced or used.

3.2   *Cook-chill* means a catering system based on the full cooking of food followed by fast chilling and storage in controlled low temperature conditions above freezing point (0°C to + 3°C) and subsequent thorough reheating close to the consumer before consumption. It can be used for up to five days including the day of cooking but not longer as food quality diminishes.

3.3   *Cook-freeze* means a catering system based on full cooking followed by fast freezing, (see 12.2) storage at controlled low temperature *conditions well below* freezing point (−18°C or below) and subsequent thorough reheating close to the consumer before prompt consumption.

3.4   Because cook-chilled products are stored above their freezing points it is essential to handle these products in accordance with the Guidelines to minimise the growth of any micro-organisms that may be present. In the case of cook-freeze products the recommended storage temperature (−18°C) is well below the freezing point of the food and so long as this storage temperature is maintained micro-organisms cannot grow.

3.5   In each system special equipment is required for rapid temperature reduction.

3.6   In both systems, initial cooking (see Section 7 below) will ensure destruction of the vegetative stages of any pathogenic micro-organisms present. Some micro-organisms produce spores which are not killed by normal cooking. Whichever system is used, the temperature range (from about +7°C to 60°C) at which these surviving organisms can readily multiply must be spanned as rapidly as possible to minimise growth during cooling, after cooking and during thawing or reheating. Detailed recommendations on these aspects of the systems are set out below (see Sections 8–15).

3.7 Most but not all non-sporing pathogens will not multiply readily below +7°C. A temperature at or below +3°C is required primarily to reduce growth of spoilage organisms and to achieve the required storage life. However, because some micro-organisms can grow at these temperatures it is strongly recommended that storage life for cook-chilled products is not greater than five days, including the day of production and the day of consumption.

3.8 In practice the storage life may be limited by considerations other than those of microbiology. For storage life of pre-cooked frozen food see 13.2.

4 NUTRITION AND FLAVOUR EFFECTS

4.1 Users should be aware that loss of nutrients occurs in cooking and at a steady rate while food is kept chilled. However, if these Guidelines are strictly observed the overall loss of nutrients from food using a cook-chill system will be kept to a minimum and should not be greater than those from alternative conventional catering systems.

4.2 RETENTION OF NUTRIENTS
The nutrient content and hence the nutritional quality of any food at the point of consumption is governed by:

i. the quality of the original raw materials;

ii. the storage conditions;

iii. the extent and nature of processing.

4.3 In particular, in any catering system, the vitamin C content of fresh vegetables decreases the longer they are held in store before preparation and in water after preparation. Optimal retention of vitamin C and other unstable nutrients occurs if the vegetables are cooked quickly and eaten as soon as possible afterwards.

4.4 *Over-cooking and prolonged delay between reheating and consumption* (see 15.1 and 15.7 for reheating and service recommendations) *reduce nutritional quality, result in loss of flavour and palatability* which can affect the acceptability and therefore the consumption of the food.

4.5 When any cooked food is frozen and stored at $-18°C$ nutrient losses occur very slowly. In addition losses occur during cooking and between reheating and consumption, and in the cook-chill process losses of nutrients also occur during the chilling process.

However, these are reduced by fast chilling. During storage of the cooked food in chilled air a number of changes due to chemical oxidation take place. Among changes observed are:

i.   some reduction in vitamin C content of vegetables when stored between 0°C and +3°C. This may vary from one vegetable to another and is most marked in the first 24 hours of storage;

ii. some other vitamins are lost to a lesser extent in the cook-chill process. Over-heating, poorly refrigerated storage and delay between re-heating and consumption adds to these vitamin losses;

iii. oxidative changes in fatty foods, particularly those of high unsaturated fatty acid content. This may result in changes in flavour due to rancidity which is more marked with longer chilled storage.

4.6   MENU SELECTION

4.6.1   It may be necessary to select menu items with lower unsaturated fatty acid content. Such items oxidise slowly and will not detract from the palatability of the meal, but care needs to be taken that the overall diet remains nutritionally sound.

4.6.2   The greatest losses in any cooking and distribution system are of vitamin C content. This can effectively be countered by the inclusion in a meal of fresh sources of vitamin C such as fresh fruit and vegetables, salads or a glass of almost any fresh fruit juice. As potatoes lose vitamin C at different rates depending on the cooking method, a choice of different forms of potato should be offered on different days eg baked, boiled, mashed, roast. This ensures better delivery of vitamin C from this important source over longer periods of time. Similarly, other vegetables lose vitamin C at different rates during cooking and cook-chill storage. It is good nutritional as well as catering practice to vary the choice of vegetables over the week to ensure the best long term delivery of this and other unstable nutrients to the consumer.

5 RAW MATERIALS

5.1 In these guidelines the term "raw materials" means all foods used as ingredients in meals, including those which have been pre-cooked.

5.2 All raw materials should be of a specified good quality. Poor quality material should be dealt with promptly through agreed procedures with the supplier and not used in the process.

5.3 The quality of incoming ingredients should be assured and controlled. This may be achieved by incorporating appropriate specifications into contracts — including full compliance with the relevant industrial codes of good manufacturing practice and by inspection of suppliers' premises by competent persons. Checks should include the conditions under which supplies are handled and enquiries should be made about suppliers' staff training in the handling of food.

6 PREPARATION AND STORAGE BEFORE COOKING

6.1   Raw materials should be stored at appropriate temperature and humidity levels so that growth of micro-organisms and loss of nutrients are minimised and general sensory quality is maintained. Suitable facilities should be provided for their storage including refrigerated storage for perishable foods and freezer storage for foodstuffs which are to be held frozen until needed. All equipment used for the temperature controlled storage of food should be provided with accurate (to ±0.5°C) thermometers so that the air temperature can be monitored. During the design stage refrigeration specialists should be asked for advice as to the most appropriate position for the thermometers and recorders.

6.2   Preparation of raw materials should take place in areas physically separated from the cooking and post-cooking areas. Frozen cooked foods should not be handled in the raw materials preparation areas. Preparation should take place on suitable working surfaces and under hygienic conditions. Particular care should be taken with raw meat, poultry and fish which should be prepared on surfaces used solely for these raw materials. To prevent transfer of micro-organisms from raw to prepared food, it is strongly recommended that personnel handling raw materials should confine themselves to the raw material area. They should not handle food or equipment in other working sections of the processing unit without changing protective clothing, washing their hands with suitable hand-cleansing agents and thoroughly drying them.

6.3   Separate machines and utensils (particularly knives) should be identified and dedicated for cooked and for raw foods and they should be situated in the appropriate area.

6.4 Special controlled thawing equipment will be necessary if frozen raw materials or pre-prepared ingredients are to be used. Such equipment should be operated in accordance with the manufacturer's instructions. Microwave equipment should not be used for thawing unless it has been specially designed to avoid uneven thawing as they are likely to leave parts of the food frozen, thus reducing the efficiency of cooking.

6.5 To facilitate cooling after cooking, it is recommended that joints of meat or packs of meat products should not exceed 2.5 kilograms in weight and 100mm in thickness or height, and that large poultry carcases should be broken down into sections not exceeding these parameters.

6.6 If quantities of food prepared for the cooking process are in excess of the available capacity of the cooking space then such prepared food should be held at temperatures below +10°C until the cooking process commences.

7 THE COOKING PROCESS

7.1 The time and temperature of the cooking should be sufficient to ensure that heat penetration to the centre of the foodstuffs will result in the destruction of non-sporing pathogens. (For nutritional considerations see Section 4 above). This is normally achieved when the centre of the food reaches a temperature of 70°C (to ensure the destruction of *Listeria monocytogenes* the temperature throughout the food should be held at above 70°C for not less than 2 minutes). It is important that the temperature is checked by inserting a probe thermometer into the slowest heating point (normally the centre) and the reading recorded.

7.2 For nutritional and microbiological reasons cooking should be automatically controlled with correct setting and siting of the sensor to ensure proper cooking. Hot holding of food after cooking should be strictly controlled see 15.1 and 15.7.

8 PREPARATION OF COOKED FOOD FOR CHILLING OR FREEZING

8.1 If pathogens contaminate cooked food they or their toxins may survive until consumption. It is therefore imperative that the strictest conditions of hygiene are observed. As the risk of contamination of food and equipment cannot be totally eliminated, handling or further treatment should be kept to a practicable minimum. Disposable gloves may be used but they do not remove the need for frequent hand washing as necessary.

8.2 When food is portioned (ie divided into smaller quantities) after cooking, this should be completed as soon as possible and in any event within 30 minutes for any product. In some installations cooked food is portioned directly from the cooking equipment eg boiling pans into multi-portion pans for immediate chilling. However, it is recommended that wherever possible any handling of food after cooking should be done in a controlled environment room with a maximum ambient temperature of +10°C.

8.3 There are several basic types of containers available for the portions of cooked food. Shallow, (50mm) re-usable stainless steel, aluminium or porcelain trays are generally suitable. All of these will allow good hygienic practices, including washing and disinfecting of containers before use. Alternatively, disposable containers can be used. These are hygienic, available in a wide variety of shapes and sizes, and are constructed of foil or fibre which has been provided with an impervious surface during manufacture. These types of container are particularly suitable where no washing-up facilities exist at the point of usage. Disposable containers should be stored under good hygienic conditions and discarded if they have become dirty or torn.

8.4 Whichever type of container is used the food should be spread as evenly as possible throughout the container and the depth be restricted to 50mm or less (but for joints of meat see 6.5) depending upon the density of the food item. A greater depth of food may be used if it has been shown that the equipment is capable of achieving an equivalent chilling time. Containers with lids have some advantage in that they can protect against contamination and will minimise dehydration of the food surface. However, lidding will add to the chilling or freezing time but must still be within the maximum time previously stated.

8.5 All equipment used should be capable of being easily cleaned and disinfected. If returnable trays are used special washing equipment should be provided and installed in a suitable area separate from food handling areas, in the production unit. Trays should be hygienically dried and stored after washing.

9 COOK — CHILL: THE CHILLING PROCESS

9.1 In order to preserve the appearance, texture, flavour, nutritional quality and safety of the cooked food, chilling should commence as soon as possible after completion of cooking (and portioning if it is done after cooking) and in any event within 30 minutes of leaving the cooker — but see 9.3 regarding large meat joints.

9.2 The food should be chilled to between 0°C and +3°C within a further period of 90 minutes. A specially designed rapid chilling apparatus is required if rapid reduction of temperature is to be achieved.

9.3 It may not be practicable to chill pieces of meat and poultry to +3°C within 90 minutes — see 6.5 for size recommendations. After cooking there are several methods of dealing with these large meats. Two possible methods are:

i. slice hot immediately after cooking then transfer the slices into a rapid chiller within 30 minutes of the joints leaving the oven. It should be noted however, that this method may cause dehydration of the slices during chilling;

ii. immediately following cooking, chill the joints. The temperature of the joints must be reduced to +10°C or below within 2½ hours of removal from the cooker. When the temperature has reached this level the joints should be sliced in a temperature controlled room immediately on a clean slicer and the slices transferred to the rapid chiller without delay.

Whichever method is used *holding times at warm temperatures should be kept to the absolute minimum to avoid serious health hazards.*

9.4 The speed of chilling of a foodstuff will also be affected by the following:

- size, shape, weight of food and construction material of the container;
- food density and moisture content;
- heat capacity of the food and the container;
- thermal conductivity of the food;
- the design of the chiller will affect chilling speed;
- temperature of the food entering the chiller;
- whether the container is provided with a cover.

9.5 In order to achieve the recommended chilling process the chiller used must have a performance specification showing it capable of reducing the temperature of a 50mm layer of food from 70°C to +3°C or below in a period not exceeding 90 minutes when *fully loaded*. This performance cannot be achieved in a storage refrigerator. With certain foods, for the reasons set out in 9.4 above, it may not be possible to achieve this temperature reduction on a 50mm layer of food; in which case the depth of the food should be reduced to allow the required performance to be achieved.

9.6 Three typical methods of chilling are:

i. the use of clean high velocity recirculating air at low temperatures in mechanical apparatus. Special mechanical chillers for liquids are available but these require appropriate cleaning and disinfection between batches;

ii. the use of cryogenic apparatus involving the use of non-oxidising gas at low temperatures;

iii. the immersion of packed products in a safe and suitable refrigerated liquid.

9.7 Whichever type of chiller is used automatic controls are required, including an accurate (±0.5°C) indicating thermometer and temperature recorder. These should be independently wired. In the mechanical type of chiller controls must hold the temperature of the food at or below +3°C until the apparatus is unloaded. Food, air, or inert gas temperatures require monitoring.

9.8 The capacity of the rapid chiller(s) must be sufficient to match peak production scheduling to ensure that rapid chilling can commence within 30 minutes of completion of cooking.

10 STORAGE OF CHILLED FOOD

10.1 The refrigerated store used for holding pre-cooked chilled foods in quantity should be specially designed for the purpose. It should allow for: access and pre-chilling of clean empty trolleys (where used); the storage of packs on shelves (as required); racking (as required) and for proper stock rotation handling methods.

10.2 In order to avoid the risk of contamination the store should be used solely for the *products of the cook-chill process*. If it were used for general purposes the more frequent opening of doors would cause unacceptable temperature fluctuations in the product. Risks of cross-contamination from other products could also arise.

10.3 The store should have a refrigeration unit capable of maintaining the products within an operational range of 0°C to +3°C.

Air temperature in the store should be measured by recording apparatus, the accuracy of which should be checked frequently. There should also be an alarm device which will indicate that the air temperature within the store has risen above acceptable operational tolerance. To avoid confusion, this device should also indicate if defrost is in operation. Remote recording at set intervals on a continuous basis of all refrigerated spaces is recommended. The recorder should preferably be located in the quality assurance or technical manager's office. Where possible temperature control alarms should be connected to points which are continuously manned such as switchboards or security offices.

10.4 An identification system should be adopted. In particular, each container of foodstuff should be conspicuously marked with the date of production and date of expiry clearly visible to and understood by all the staff who may handle the food.

10.5 A strict system of stock control should be operated so that stored foods are consumed in proper sequence. Should any food in the store exceed the agreed expiry date it should be regarded as unsuitable for consumption and destroyed.

11 TIME AND TEMPERATURE LIMITATIONS IN STORAGE AND DISTRIBUTION OF CHILLED FOODS

11.1 As mentioned at 3.4 above chilled foods are much more vulnerable to temperature abuse during storage than frozen foods. It is therefore essential that the following limits are observed:

i. the temperature of the cooked food after chilling should be maintained at or below +3°C throughout the entire storage and distribution (including holding in vending machines) until reheating. An increase in product temperature to +5°C may be permitted for very short periods of time eg when on defrost cycles;

ii. where the temperature requirements are achieved the maximum life of the cooked products should not exceed 5 days including both the day of cooking and the day of consumption — this also applies where pre-cooked chilled products are purchased from outside suppliers;

iii. should the temperature of the cooked food during storage and distribution and before reheating exceed +5°C but not +10°C, the food should be consumed as soon as possible and in any case within 12 hours of this temperature abuse. If not it should be destroyed;

iv. Should the temperature of the cooked food during storage and distribution and before reheating exceed +10°C the food should be regarded as unsuitable for use and should be destroyed;

v. the system is intended to hold food at or below +3°C. It must be clearly understood that *the tolerances contained in i. and iii. above are not alternative systems of holding cook chill food allowing batches of food to be kept at higher temperatures for shorter times.*

12 COOK-FREEZE: THE FREEZING PROCESS

12.1 The freezing should commence as soon as possible after completion of cooking and portioning and in any event within 30 minutes of leaving the cooker — for large joints and poultry see 6.5 for size recommendations and 9.3 for slicing procedure. Following slicing the meat to be frozen should be dealt with as below.

12.2 The food should reach a centre temperature of at least −5°C within 90 minutes of entering the freezer and subsequently should reach a storage temperature of −18°C.

12.3 Food that has thawed either partially or completely should not be refrozen. Food that has thawed at unknown temperatures should not be used for human consumption.

12.4 Whichever type of freezing unit is used automatic monitoring controls will be required. An accurate external indicator will be necessary to show the internal air temperature of the freezer.

13 STORAGE OF PRE-COOKED FROZEN FOODS

13.1 Pre-cooked frozen food should be stored at − 18°C or below. Air temperature measurement recording with 'alarm' devices should be as specified in 10.3 for chilled food.

13.2 The shelf-life of pre-cooked frozen food varies according to the type of food but in general it may be stored for up to 8 weeks without any significant loss of nutrients or palatability. After that time rancidity may develop in foods with a high fat content, but other foods can be satisfactorily stored for longer periods. Nevertheless, a clear system of marking the containers with product identification, batch and production date and expiry date should be operated so that stock can be rotated on a first-in/first-out basis.

14 DISTRIBUTION OF PRE-COOKED CHILLED AND PRE-COOKED FROZEN FOOD

PRIMARY DISTRIBUTION — FROM CENTRAL PRODUCTION UNITS TO SATELLITE KITCHENS

14.1 The distribution of *chilled foods* is the most difficult part of the process to control effectively in terms of temperature fluctuation. It is essential that the temperature does not rise above the designated storage temperature of the food, as stated in paragraph 11.1.i., particularly if the storage period is to be extended (up to the maximum) at the consumer outlet after distribution.

14.2 Pre-cooked *frozen food* is often subject to a further frozen storage period after distribution. This should only be permitted if no part of the frozen food has thawed. If the food is to be further stored the temperature must be returned rapidly to −18°C or below.

14.3 Where the distribution period is very short and is to be followed by immediate reheating and consumption, insulated containers may be adequate for temperature preservation although the temperature rise which occurs in such situations should be regularly monitored. Insulated containers should be chilled before use. It is recommended that distribution containers or vehicles should be refrigerated where the distribution period is prolonged, when ambient air temperatures are high and where distribution is to be followed by further storage in refrigerated stores at the consumer outlet.

14.4 There are several types of refrigeration systems used on vehicles which are suitable:

i. an insulated vehicle in which cold CO_2 gas derived from solid CO_2 is circulated;

      ii.   an insulated vehicle in which cold nitrogen gas derived from liquid nitrogen is circulated;

      iii.   an insulated vehicle in which cold air from a mechanical refrigerated unit is circulated;

      iv.   an insulated vehicle which is fitted with eutectic plates pre-chilled or frozen prior to the use of the vehicle.

14.5   The manufacturers stated specification of the vehicle capability may need to be supported by test reports.

SECONDARY DISTRIBUTION — TO CONSUMERS

14.6   This section refers to distribution of *chilled* and *frozen* meals from either the central production unit to consumers or from satellite units to consumers.

14.7   The meals or meal components will be held in storage units as described in Sections 11 and 13. In *installations such as hospitals it is necessary to transport the chilled or frozen food from a central cold store to points of re-heating before consumption eg wards*. Distribution trolleys are available with facilities for maintaining the cold chain during transport. At the ward the trolley is connected to an electric supply which rapidly raises the centre temperature of the food to 70°C.

14.8   In these installations there are two main methods of distributing *chilled* meals. Either the chilled food in the bulk trays is plated cold and distributed under chill or the bulk trays are distributed under chill, reheated at the point of consumption and plated hot for immediate service. Where cold plating is carried out it is recommended that this is done in a separate room under controlled conditions using either air surrounding the food at a maximum of +10°C or other means of maintaining the food within the limits stated at 11.1.

15 REHEATING AND SERVICE

15.1 Under no circumstances should the food be reheated at a single central point and distributed hot unless distribution times are less than 15 minutes to the commencement of service. Failure to observe this defeats the basic objective of the cook-chill and cook-freeze systems.

15.2 Reheating of the food should take place at or close to the point of consumption. Frozen and chilled food that has been re-heated is as vulnerable as conventionally prepared food to contamination and loss of nutritional quality and palatability.

15.3 Reheating of chilled food should begin as soon as possible and no longer than 30 minutes after the food is removed from chill (either bulk chill, secondary chill or chilled trolley). For reasons of safety and palatability the centre temperature of the food should reach at least 70°C and be maintained at not less than 70°C for 2 minutes.

15.4 Some types of frozen foods such as cold desserts, need only be thawed to chill temperatures for serving. Other foods may need to be thawed before reheating. For food hygiene reasons thawing should be kept separate from other operations. Temperature rise should be carefully controlled, if possible automatically, so as to achieve the desired temperature in the minimum time possible.

15.5 Thawed food should be held at or below +3°C and never above +10°C until reheated. Food thawed in rapid thaw cabinets should be consumed within 24 hours.

15.6 Suitable types of reheating equipment include infra-red units, forced air and steamer convection ovens and special chill/reheat trolleys. Traditional types of hot air ovens may be used but tend to dehydrate exposed areas of the food during reheating. Recipes are usually designed to allow a standard time and temperature to be used for the final reheating of all foods. The reheating should operate automatically to give the required time and temperature, with humidification where appropriate, as the nutritional quality and palatability of the food can be impaired by overheating. Food that has been reheated and allowed to cool should be destroyed.

15.7   For quality reasons, following reheating to 70°C, service of the food should commence as soon as possible and within 15 minutes of reheating. The temperature must not be allowed to fall below 63°C.

15.8   Foods intended to be eaten cold or at room temperature should be consumed as soon as possible and preferably within 30 minutes of removal from chilled storage.

15.9   *It is essential that any meals not consumed should be destroyed and not reheated or returned to chilled storage.*

16 MANAGEMENT OF QUALITY ASSURANCE

ESTABLISHING A SYSTEM

16.1 Because health hazards will arise if the principles in these Guidelines are not carefully followed, a strict system of quality assurance of a production schedule for each menu item should be established and enforced at all times. It is recommended that this system adopts the hazard analysis critical control point (HACCP) approach. This will require input from technically competent personnel capable of identifying the critical control points in the system, establishing appropriate monitoring procedures for those points and appropriate training for all staff concerned with food production. In large operations this may be best achieved by appointing a quality assurance manager. For HACCP to be fully effective a corporate approach involving personnel from all the disciplines and crafts involved is essential.

ACTION ON DEVIATIONS

16.2 If, during the monitoring of the critical control points, deviations from the established criteria are identified they should be highlighted in the record and the production manager informed immediately so that corrective action can be taken and the unsafe product condemned.

ESSENTIAL CONTROL CHECKS

16.3 The following parameters should be checked and recorded for every batch and menu item processed:

i. the quality, and the temperature where appropriate, of the raw materials;

ii. the temperature at which perishable raw and pre-cooked materials are stored prior to preparation for cooking;

iii. the centre temperatures of meat and poultry during cooking;

iv. the period which elapses during the portioning process;

v. the period which elapses during the cooling process of large pieces of meat and poultry;

vi. the time of the chilling or freezing process for portioned foods and the centre temperature of the food at the completion of the chilling process;

vii. the temperature of the chilling/freezing medium;

viii. the temperature of the food during storage and the air temperature of the chill freezer store as recorded on the automatic recording instrument;

ix. the rotation of stocks within the store;

x. the temperature of the food at the completion of its distribution from the refrigerated store;

xi. the centre temperatures achieved during the reheating process for each type of food which is subjected to a treatment prior to consumption.

TEMPERATURE MEASUREMENT AND MONITORING

16.4 An adequate number of electronic thermometers, with a selection of probes, should be available for monitoring the temperature control points indicated above and any additional points identified in the HACCP. Precautions should be taken against transferring micro-organisms from raw to cooked material by temperature probes — separate probes should be used and they should be wiped and disinfected after each use.

16.5 The temperature of the food will not necessarily be the same as that of the surrounding air or cryogenic gas. Some temperature variations are likely to occur at different points in the processes. All records of temperatures and other monitoring results at critical control points should be kept for at least three months. Indications of temperature abuse should be investigated and corrected promptly.

MICROBIOLOGICAL GUIDELINES

16.6 The following microbiological guidelines are not intended to be used for routine testing of batches of food and are not the standards for the acceptance or rejection of any batch. Rather they should be used when setting up a new cook-chill or cook-freeze installation or when making alterations to processes or procedures to provide assurance that a satisfactory product can be provided.

16.7 Detailed microbiological surveillance may be important in assuring that the procedures established locally are satisfactory. Thereafter strict control of the operation with particular attention to monitoring of the critical control points (which may on occasions include microbiological checks of raw materials, food contact surfaces and equipment) is the most reliable means of achieving product safety. Occasional checks of finished products against these guidelines may be undertaken at the discretion of the persons responsible (see 16.8). Considerable differences must be expected between various types of foods. Failure to meet the limits given in the following paragraph does not mean that the batch of food should necessarily be condemned; it does however, indicate that a thorough check should be made of all stages in the process and *if there is any doubt the food should be destroyed,* apart from samples for further testing.

16.8 It is suggested that one sample of about 100 grammes of each item of food be taken from each batch tested. The samples should be taken immediately before the food is due to be reheated so that the results reflect any abuse conditions to which the item sampled has been subjected during storage and transport following processing. Advice from the local microbiologists or PHLS should be sought to ensure samples are taken properly. Food should generally achieve the following microbiological criteria:

> Total aerobic colony count after incubation of agar plates for 48 hours at 37°C — less than 100,000 per gramme.
>
> *Salmonella* species — not detected in 25 grammes.
>
> *Escherichia coli* — less than 10 per gramme.
>
> *Staphylococcus aureus* (coagulase positive) less than 100 per gramme.
>
> *Clostridium perfringens* less than 100 per gramme.
>
> *Listeria monocytogenes* — not detected in 25 grammes.

NOTE: Variations in the total aerobic colony count are the most useful guide to the hygiene and temperature control of the processes.

16.9   These criteria apply to cooked chilled and frozen food therefore they will be affected by the quality of the raw materials and the standards of cooking, handling, chilling or freezing and chill/frozen storage. They are not intended to be applied to the food once it has been re-heated.

17 MAINTENANCE

17.1 Thermometers, temperature recording devices, refrigerators, chillers, freezers, automatic cooking equipment and other devices and equipment should be checked and maintained regularly.

17.2 Accuracy of thermometers should be examined every three months, against a certified thermometer.

BIBLIOGRAPHY

1. CAMPDEN FOOD AND DRINK RESEARCH ASSOCIATION
Guidelines to the establishment of hazard analysis critical control point (HACCP). Technical Manual No 19 1987 Campden Food and Drink Research Association, Chipping Campden, Glos GL55 6LD.

2. DHSS Health Service Catering Hygiene 1987 HMSO.

3. CHARLES R H G, Mass Catering 1983 WHO Regional Publications, European Services No 15 WHO, Regional Office for Europe, Copenhagen ISBN 92 890 11068.

4. BOGNAR A, Nutritive Value of Chilled Meals (p307-407) In: "Advances in Catering Technology" Ed. G Glew. 1985. Elsevier Applied Science Publishers.

5. MAFF "The Manual of Nutrition" 9th Edition London HMSO 1985.

6. INTERNATIONAL COMMISSION ON MICROBIOLOGICAL SPECIFICATIONS FOR FOODS
Application of the hazard analysis critical control point (HACCP) system to ensure microbiological safety and quality 1988. Blackwell Scientific Publications

7. Food Hygiene (General) Regulations 1970.